...a season of
Gladness

a season of

Gladness

ELIZABETH M. HOEKSTRA

WITH THE WATERCOLORS OF MARLENE MᶜLOUGHLIN

CROSSWAY BOOKS • WHEATON, ILLINOIS
A DIVISION OF GOOD NEWS PUBLISHERS

A Season of Gladness

Copyright © 2000 by Elizabeth M. Hoekstra

Published by Crossway Books
> a division of Good News Publishers
> 1300 Crescent Street
> Wheaton, Illinois 60187

Cover and interior illustrations: Marlene McLoughlin

Book Design: Liita Forsyth

Hand-tooled leather for cover: Bob Roberts

First printing 2000

Printed in the United States of America

Library of Congress Cataloging-in-Publication Data
Hoekstra, Elizabeth M. 1962-
  A season of gladness / Elizabeth M. Hoekstra.
    p.   cm. (All creation sings)
    ISBN 1-58134-205-5 (alk. paper)
    1. Meditations. 2. Spring—Religious aspects—Christianity—Meditations.
I. Title.
BV4832.2.H594   2000
242—dc21   00-009047
                                    CIP

15	14	13	12	11	10	09	08	07	06	05	04	03	02	01	00
15	14	13	12	11	10	9	8	7	6	5	4	3	2	1	

Dedication

To the ones I nurture
and who offer me
a hundredfold return on my investment:
my husband, Peter,
and our children,
Geneva and Jordan

In the rebirth of the fields and forests every spring on my family's small New Hampshire farm I find many parallels with a person's walk with God. In the following meditations I invite you to take a journey through the planting season God invests in each of us. My prayer is that you'll feel refreshed by the transparency of our family: Peter, my husband, our children, Geneva and Jordan, and myself.

Come Walk with Us

WHERE WERE YOU when I laid the earth's foundation? Tell me, if you understand. Who marked off its dimensions? Surely you know! Who stretched a
measuring line across it? On what were its footings set, or who laid its corner-
stone—while the morning stars sang together and all the angels shouted for joy?
Who shut up the sea behind closed doors when it burst forth from the womb,
when I made the clouds its garment and wrapped it in thick darkness, when I
fixed limits for it and set its doors and bars in place, when I said, "This far
you may come and no farther; here is where your proud waves halt"? Have
you ever given orders to the morning, or shown dawn its place?

Job 38:4-12

The Lord Is the Source of Wisdom

He founded the world by his wisdom
and stretched out the heavens by his understanding.

JEREMIAH 10:12b

Take a Faith Walk

Fix these words of mine in your hearts and minds …
Teach them to your children, talking about them when you
sit at home and when you walk along the road.

DEUTERONOMY 11:18-19a

LATE EACH AFTERNOON in the spring, my children and I walk or ride bikes down our dirt road. They need the exercise to release tension from school; I need the exercise to wake up. When we start out, the kids might ask, "How far are we going?" We then decide to either stop at the bridge a half mile away or go the full mile to the end of the road where the pavement begins. There we can collect the daily paper from our newspaper box.

As we crunch along, we stop to look at animal tracks impressed into the soft dirt along the gravel road edge. The tracks range from the wide, deep prints of bear or moose to the tiniest prints of birds, mice, and chipmunks. We also look overhead and speculate about which leaves—the elm or the oak—are nearly full. We stop at the bridge over the brook and look for tadpoles while we talk about how they metamorphose into frogs.

By the time my children were five, they could easily discern a deer track from a moose's, a dog track from a fox's, a mouse track from a chipmunk's. These are things I taught them. Why? Because of my belief that an interest in nature is inborn and only remains alive if nurtured. Over the years my footfalls on our walks often step in time with the above Scripture: "Teach them to your children, talking about them … when you walk along the road." I'm always looking for opportunities to teach my children to have a respect for nature and about the parallels between nature and their faith walks.

How will children learn to admire the earth that the Lord has entrusted to us if we don't teach them? This week consider taking a walk with a child. Pray for lessons you can share with him or her. If you don't have children of your own at home, you can walk with a neighbor's or a friend's child. Meditate on this verse as you walk: "The earth is the LORD's, and everything in it, the world, and all who live in it" (Ps. 24:1).

MORE SCRIPTURE FOR STUDY:
Genesis 1:20-28; Numbers 35:34;
Psalm 19:1-4; 2 John 4

Enough for Today

Give us today our daily bread.

MATTHEW 6:11

MAKING BREAD FROM SCRATCH is a satisfying, cathartic activity. Into warm water I mix molasses, oatmeal, butter, and salt. I add flour and the essential ingredient of yeast. Then comes the best part: kneading the thick dough. Finally the dough is shaped to rise twice before baking.

I don't make bread even once a week. But some mornings when I awake, I just know: *This is a bread-making day.* Maybe I'm feeling some pent-up frustration and need to pound it out on the kneading board. Maybe I feel a need to create and complete a project. Maybe I simply want to draw my family to the dinner table with the promise of good food and pleasant company.

"Give us today our daily bread." Bread for today. Jesus told His disciples that all they needed to pray for was bread for *today*. Nourishment for *today*. Strength for *today*. Is He talking just about actual food? Maybe He's gently reminding us that there are some "breads" with which we need to continuously refill our souls.

What spiritual "bread" do you need to ingest every day? Patience with

16

your children? Tenderness with your spouse? Compassion with your neighbors? "Give us *today* our daily bread." You may need to ask for the same breads of grace tomorrow, but start by asking for today. He'll give you enough for today. Don't worry about tomorrow. Think about what the Lord told Moses while the Israelites traveled in the wilderness: "'I will rain down bread from heaven for you. The people are to go out each day and gather enough for that day'" (Exod. 16:4).

MORE SCRIPTURE FOR STUDY:
Exodus 16:1-18; Deuteronomy 8:3;
Matthew 7:7-12; John 6:25-59

Amisfield Farm

You are God's field, God's building.

1 CORINTHIANS 3:9b

EVERY FARM—even a nonprofit one like ours—has a name. When we bought our home, Peter and I thought about various names that could speak of our lives, our property, and even our heritage. We finally settled on Amisfield Farm. The name Amisfield came from my great-aunt's home in Scotland where her property housed a tower (Amisfield Tower) that was used during the border wars between England and Scotland. Peter and I had visited her homestead before we were married and loved the brick farmhouse, the round, five-story stone watchtower, and the rock walls edging the rolling fields. It all looked vast, open, and wildly beautiful—exactly what we wanted our farm to become.

Of course, a problem presented itself from the start. Most of our property was wooded. The name of our farm took on a more subtle meaning: "Aim is field" Farm. Our aim was to cut back the trees and reclaim the open land in fields.

It seems that the Lord applied the name and goal of our farm straight to my heart too. "Aim is field." His aim and plan for my life parallels my aim for our property. He wants my heart to be open. He wants my heart to have fertile soil. He wants my heart to be ready to receive the seeds of faith that I need to nurture. He wants those seeds to grow to a full harvest that will yield an abundance for Him.

How about you? Can you too say that His aim for you is a field for Him to plant? At what stage is He right now in your heart? Is He cutting the old, twisted trees from your spirit? Maybe He's pulling stumps and rocks from your soul. How about tilling up poor attitudes or spreading fertilizer? This week, talk with the Lord about the field He is preparing in your heart:

My aim, Lord, is a field in my heart for You to plant.

MORE SCRIPTURE FOR STUDY:
Matthew 13:1-9, 18-23; Ephesians 2:10;
2 Timothy 2:21

Clearing Fields

As the terebinth and oak leave stumps when they are cut down,
so the holy seed will be the stump in the land.

ISAIAH 6:13

WHAT DO YOU SUPPOSE HAPPENS IF, after a patch of land is cleared, the remaining stumps aren't removed right away? Within a year they sprout, sending several hardy shoots straight up. After all, there's a vast, well-established root structure underneath the stump, ready to support new life through and on top of it.

Peter and I learned all of this the hard and expensive way on "Aim is field" Farm. We waited three years between clear-cutting a three-acre lot and stumping it. By the time we brought in a bulldozer and backhoe, the shoots attached to the stumps were nearly wrist thick. The lesson we learned? Cutting off the top of a tree doesn't kill the bottom of the tree.

This lesson is exactly what the above verse describes. Why would the remaining stump be called the "holy seed"? Because new life springs from it. The "holy seed" stump can only be Jesus. Just as a cut-off oak regenerates, new life would spring up in the form of the "holy seed" of Christ despite Israel's destruction.

The same is true in our hearts. First, we may undergo radical cutting and pruning of our hearts to prepare a usable field. Second, we see the promise of the "stump" that will always remain in our hearts: His Spirit. "He anointed us, set his seal of ownership on us, and put his spirit in our hearts as a deposit, guaranteeing what is to come" (2 Cor. 1:21b-22).

Even as He reworks (sometimes painfully) your heart to prime it for seeding, will you thank Him for the promise of His "holy seed" deeply embedded in your soul?

MORE SCRIPTURE FOR STUDY:
2 Samuel 7:27-29; Ecclesiastes 3:11;
Matthew 10:28; Philippians 1:6

Be Prepared

She sees that her trading is profitable, and her lamp
does not go out at night.

PROVERBS 31:18

PREPAREDNESS IS A TRADEMARK of the Yankee spirit. It's an inheritance from our ancestors. New Englanders know how to anticipate and prepare for everything. We don't live in the tomorrow; we just plan for it. We can fruit in the fall; we freeze vegetables in the summer; we cut, chop, and stack wood for cold winters; we stuff money under the mattress; we save everything … just in case. (I'm convinced that's why New England barns are so big—just for storage of *stuff.*) We call this preparedness Yankee frugality and ingenuity.

As much as I may make fun of my heritage, having a prepared heart and home really is a virtue. It reminds me of the Proverbs 31 woman. (Men can learn something from this role model, even if she only serves as a reminder for them to pray for their wives to become more like this highly ideal woman!) The verse above tells us that "her lamp does not go out at night." Does this mean she never sleeps? It doesn't seem likely. Lack of sleep would diminish her ability to carry out her multiple tasks during the day. Perhaps this verse has a deeper meaning about preparedness. She makes sure that she has oil to keep her lamp burning.

Taking these thoughts even deeper, I believe we also learn about her *inner light*—the light of the Lord in her life. Her "lamp" does not grow dim at the moment of threatened spiritual darkness. It keeps shining through the dark times in her life and home. The light of her prepared heart keeps shining even when she's threatened by the darkness of discouragement, fatigue, feeling overwhelmed, anger, disappointment, sadness, etc.

In what ways can you prepare for spiritual nighttime? Take a lesson from New Englanders and the Proverbs 31 woman: be prepared by storing up God's Word in your heart to keep your light shining through the night. "You, O LORD, keep my lamp burning; my God turns my darkness into light" (Ps. 18:28).

MORE SCRIPTURE FOR STUDY:
Psalm 119:105; Luke 12:35;
2 Timothy 4:1-5; 1 Peter 1:13; 5:8-10

Blooming in New Places

As for man, his days are like grass, he flourishes
like a flower of the field.

PSALM 103:15

ONE OF THE EARLIEST SPRING FLOWERS in New England is the forsythia bush. The delicate yellow flowers have four tiny petals standing upright next to one another.

As a child I caught my mother's enthusiasm in watching for the unfolding of the forsythia. In childlike innocence I thought the flower's name was "for Cynthia"—meaning the flower carried my mother's name and was indeed just for her.

In early spring, when the forsythia bush buds in little brown shells at the tips of its branches, the leggy stalks can be cut and put in water in a warm place. Within a week, the buds will burst and the yellow flowers will start to unfurl. This blooming takes place while there may still be frost in the air outside and perhaps a month before the flowers on the bushes burst open naturally.

This "forcing" process sounds a little like us at times, doesn't it? Sometimes the Lord takes us out of our natural element—our "comfort zone"—and sets us in a new place. We may be certain that we'll wither since we've been taken out of our usual environment. But just as I put my flowers in a vase in the sun on the kitchen table, God places us where we'll bloom. We think we can't possibly bloom in this new environment. ("What, me go on a mission trip to a foreign country?") The situations where we are out of our natural element force us to rely solely on the Lord. Then He can really do some fast work! Through the forcing process we bloom more quickly than we ever thought possible.

Have you felt a little out of your element lately? Has the Lord placed you in a hot spot where you are uncertain about your role? Can you rest in the confidence that He will give you the grace to bloom even outside of your comfort zone?

MORE SCRIPTURE FOR STUDY:
Exodus 4:1-17; John 15:16;
2 Corinthians 9:8; 12:9; Philippians 1:6

A Time of Rest

The land itself must observe a Sabbath to the LORD....
The land is to have a year of rest.

LEVITICUS 25:2-5

WISE FARMERS KNOW the benefits of letting a field "rest" for a season. Lying fallow allows the field to replenish lost nutrients and restore its resources. Farmers may even give the soil's pH balance a boost with fertilizer or lime.

What happens in overworked fields that can't be spared from producing a cash crop? The earth becomes "run out." The soil has been stripped of its valuable nutrients and minerals. Any crop planted will grow weaker and produce a lower yield.

Is this starting to sound familiar? We too find ourselves depleted of valuable resources. Where do I see this in my life? In fatigue that won't go away, stress weighting my shoulders, or the feeling of being overwhelmed. Need I say more? How do we get this way? Overcommitment, long days with not enough sleep, and weekends spent playing "catch-up." Our spiritual and personal resources are taxed. Like the fields, our "yield" is lower.

The Lord instructed the Israelites to give their fields a year off every seventh year. We can apply this principle to our personal spiritual fields too. We need time off to replenish our spirits with lasting nutrients. When we do take time off, we'll have more energy, a better focus, and ultimately will produce a more plentiful harvest.

Are there areas in your life where you feel depleted? Maybe you've led a Bible study or served on a committee for several years and need a break. Will you look at your schedule for the coming weeks and months and pray about areas where you can lie fallow for a time? The Lord wants you full of the energy required for His service. This spring your mission may be to find time to rest in Him as He refills you.

MORE SCRIPTURE FOR STUDY:
Ecclesiastes 3:1-9; Isaiah 32:18; 57:10;
Matthew 11:28-30

Submission

Submit yourselves, then, to God.... Humble yourselves
before the LORD, and he will lift you up.

JAMES 4:7-10

IT'S BEEN SAID that some aspects of nature reflect the spiritual life. In the twelve years that I've been training my Morgan horse, Galilee, I've relived over and over the parallels between training him and my personal growth. When he makes mistakes, there are consequences, while good choices produce rewards (carrots). For both of us, learning through repetition and experience creates a balanced, more mature individual.

When I began riding Galilee as a three-year-old, he would leap for no reason—at least no reason discernible to me. His jumps scared me. All four feet would leave the ground as he launched himself forward, ignoring my restraining hand. His flight instinct was stronger than his need to obey my authority. Over the next several years I gently and frequently reminded him of the unacceptable nature of his actions. He slowly learned to accept my instruction as a form of protection for both of us.

Sounds like us, doesn't it? Like a young opinionated horse, sometimes we take the guiding reins and leap in rebellion. Perhaps it takes a decisive correction from our Master to remind us just Who is in charge. His steady hands on the reins of our lives are there to support us and guide us, not harm us.

Why does the Lord want our obedience? To protect us. If we're disobedient, we're in a double crisis: we're outside of His protection and are ripe for chastening. Without His gentle hands leading us, we could wander off, oblivious to lurking dangers. Submission to the Lord's direction means safety. Are you willing to release any rebellious tendencies to the Lord?

MORE SCRIPTURE FOR STUDY:
Isaiah 1:18-19; John 6:45; 12:32;
Romans 13:1-3; James 1:22-24

Long Growing Seasons

Being strengthened with all power according to his glorious might
so that you might have great endurance and patience.

COLOSSIANS 1:11

GROWING ASPARAGUS TAKES three years from seed planting to edible harvest. That sounds like so long! During the drawn-out maturation process the soil must be tended, nutrients added, and winter cover given. How frustrating for an impatient gardener like me! I don't even bother to plant asparagus because I can't bear the fact that they aren't "done" within one growing season.

I wonder if the Lord feels frustrated when we aren't "done yet" too. The problem is that we think we're ready long before the Lord has finished growing us. We get impatient and whine, "Aren't You done with me *yet* about this issue, Lord?" Sometimes His answer is, "No, you have more growing to do. I want to see you a little straighter, a little taller, a little fuller in your faith."

Are there areas in your life in which you have felt your patience stretched to the breaking point? What are some things you have felt impatient for? A home of your own? The perfect job? An improved relationship? Some delays occur because something else in our lives may need working on. In other words, that other area isn't "done yet." Who knows—maybe by the time we're "ready," we would have grown so much in patience that what we were waiting for won't seem as important anymore. Maybe that's when we'll be "done" in the Lord's eyes.

I think I'm going to plant asparagus this spring.

MORE SCRIPTURE FOR STUDY:
Romans 8:25; 2 Corinthians 12:7-10;
Colossians 1:3-14; 2 Peter 3:8-9

The Kind Shepherd

Your rod and your staff, they comfort me.

PSALM 23:4

GROWING UP ON A SMALL FARM, we had two pet sheep. My sisters and I raised them and named them Tigerlily and Daffodil. (Need I say this was back in the early '70s?) Tiger and Daffy, as they were affectionately called, started as mostly black sheep and slowly turned gray over the years. Though we weren't connoisseurs of fleece, we had been told that their wool was highly desirable for weaving and knitting.

In the spring of each year, a traveling sheepshearer came to our home to shear the wool off of Daffy and Tiger. The only problem with shearing a sheep is that you can't reason with it about getting shorn. A sheep doesn't understand the benefit—feeling cooler—of getting shorn.

Here is what we learned through that experience. First, the reluctant creature has to be caught. She is then flipped to a half-sitting position—not a natural posture for a sheep. She'll wiggle, leap, and flail her sharp hooves. But once the sheep is entirely on her back, she'll stop struggling. That's her most vulnerable position—belly exposed to a perceived threat. Has she submitted because she reasons that's the best thing to do to prevent injury to herself or others? Not likely. Sheep are notoriously unintelligent. No, she's simply given up.

I've often wondered why Jesus compared people to sheep. Is it because we're not very bright? Or did He use the comparison because He knew that we submit only when pushed hard enough? Maybe His reasoning involved a combination of both. We need a kind Shepherd who can steady us under His knowledgeable hands as He works to rid us of heavy baggage.

"I am the good shepherd; I know my sheep and my sheep know me" (John 10:14). What does this verse tell us? He knows us. He recognizes us—inside and out. He knows our need for His leadership. And, most importantly, He is good to us.

MORE SCRIPTURE FOR STUDY:
Psalms 23; 100:3; Isaiah 40:11;
John 10:1-18

Setting Sail

Your rigging hangs loose: The mast is not held secure,
the sail is not spread.

ISAIAH 33:23a

THERE SEEMS TO BE nothing sadder at a boat dock than a sailing craft stripped of its dignity. The halyards slap noisily against the mast. The slack lines trail over the deck and into the water where green algae grows near their once-white knots. The frayed sails piled on deck have black mold and mildew spots. The entire ship looks disheartened and abandoned.

I've seen boats like this in harbors along the Atlantic. They wear defeated looks because they are not being used for what they were created to do—sail.

There are times when we also have that same defeated look—times when our bodies feel limp like unused sails and our minds seem stagnant because of self-doubt. Any move we make is only in response to what is going on around us. We might also feel that we've lost our perspective.

What can we do when the winter doldrums carry over into spring? If we were repairing a sailing craft to return to sailing, we'd tackle the jobs one at a time. The same is true for our spiritual lives. Maybe the first job is to clean off the lines of communication we have with the Lord. That means confessing and repenting of any sin that the Holy Spirit brings to mind.

As you start to tidy up, think about leaving the dock where you've been held fast. What is your destination? Perhaps it is a quiet bay where your sail can catch some wind, a place where you can be or do what you were created to do—minister in your areas of giftedness. Can you help out in the church nursery rocking little babies? Can you cook a meal for an elderly neighbor? Can you help organize a friend's office? Using your gifts takes the focus off you and puts it onto the Lord. It also frees you from stagnation.

Won't you decide to set sail this spring?

MORE SCRIPTURE FOR STUDY:
Psalm 116:16; Matthew 25:14-30;
1 Corinthians 12

Waiting for Heaven

Do you know when the mountain goats give birth? ...
Do you count the months till they bear?
Do you know the time they give birth?

JOB 39:1-2

IT SEEMED AN ENDLESS ELEVEN-MONTH wait until my mare, Foxfyre, gave birth to her long-anticipated foal. When Galilee finally came into the world on April 21, he immediately stretched his legs, stood up, and wobbled to his mother's udder. Though I watched from the stall doorway, I didn't offer him any help. He worked on his own instincts, as did his mother who licked and gently nipped him. The wait was finally over.

Wouldn't you like to know how the Lord determined the gestation period of mammals? Mice and small critters only gestate for a few weeks, puppies for sixteen weeks, and elephants for two years—whew! And humans think nine months is long. Imagine being pregnant for two years!

Yet the Lord determined the gestation time and process for a reason. Some would say the length of the human gestation period was determined because it takes nine months for humans to adjust to the idea of being a parent. But I believe the wait has more to do with teaching us patience and the rewards of anticipation.

Our twenty-first-century world is full of instant gratification: drive-through windows for food, medicines, money, etc.; remote-controlled TVs, VCRs, DVD players, and garage-door openers; lottery tickets for instant prizes. We don't want to wait. We've also forgotten the thrill of anticipation in many instances.

What do we anticipate? In the short term we might anticipate the coming of a baby, a new job, a more secure future, a vacation, etc. When the wait is over, we feel relief, satisfaction, or joy. But what about the long term? What are all Christians waiting for? Jesus' return. Our eternal home in heaven. That's why, I believe, we're given times of waiting here on earth. At the end of each waiting period, we're given a tiny glimpse of the eternal, complete joy of heaven.

Will you wait with joyful anticipation of what the Lord has prepared for us in heaven? Let these words encourage you while you wait: "Take your inheritance, the kingdom prepared for you since the creation of the world" (Matt. 25:34).

MORE SCRIPTURE FOR STUDY:
Exodus 23:20; Jeremiah 29:11;
John 14:1-4; Romans 8:18-25

The Lord Is Merciful

The LORD your God is a merciful God;
he will not abandon or destroy you.

DEUTERONOMY 4:31

One Free Thing

Cursed is the ground because of you; through painful toil
you will eat of it all the days of your life.

GENESIS 3:17

BASED ON THE ABOVE VERSE, it seems that the problems often encountered in farming and gardening are part of the curse that resulted from sin. Prior to Adam and Eve's sin they did not have to labor for their food. It lay conveniently at their fingertips. But after their banishment from the Garden of Eden, they had to learn how to work the earth.

The "toil" part of the verse dictates our lives now. Even the ground itself was affected by the Fall. It too must work. The soil "works" to sustain new life, protect root systems, produce food, etc.

The "ground" the verse speaks of also can be seen as the ground of our spirits. "Painful toil" in our lives reminds us that everything—food, relationships, children, money—requires an effort of some sort. The curse spoken of is the effort these resources of life require. The things themselves aren't curses. We just can't enjoy them unabashedly without some form of "toil" to sustain them.

This is why the free gift from God (forgiveness from sin) is so remarkable. Our lives are spent in toil; yet none of our efforts will gain us entrance to heaven. Our open door to heaven is through the free, unconditional gift of forgiveness when we believe that God's only Son died on the cross for our sins. He offers no choice in the necessity of laboring on the earth to sustain living; yet He gave one free choice: Jesus.

As you tend your garden or yard this spring or admire other people's gardens, reflect on how all of the earth must "work." We can be thankful we don't have to work to receive Christ's forgiveness. We only have to ask.

MORE SCRIPTURE FOR STUDY:
Isaiah 55:7; John 3:16-17;
Romans 3:21-26; 2 Thessalonians 3:8-13

Peace in the Storm

*His thunder announces the coming storm; even
the cattle make known its approach.*

JOB 36:33

HAVE YOU HEARD that birds stop singing before tornadoes? Did you know that dogs whimper and pace restlessly when a storm approaches and cows lie down when rain is forecast?

Cattle are like living barometers. When they feel the pressure drop, they lie down. The rain sheds harmlessly off their backs, while their undersides stay warm and dry. They nonchalantly lie and chew their cud. That's the instinct God provided them.

How about us? What do we do when a storm is brewing? It would seem foolish to just lie down like the cows. That may seem to us too much like giving up. But think again about it. Cows don't run back to the supposed safety of the barn. They must feel pretty secure to just plop down where they've been grazing. They rest securely right where they are (Ps. 16:9).

Storms have blown in fast and furiously in my life. At other times they mounted up gradually. How about in your life? Do you feel threatened by the

42

winds of job loss, debts, unexpected pregnancies, children gone astray, strained family relationships, abuse, illness, and so on? These storms might be brief squalls or full-blown, life-damaging blasts. When trials come, can you take a lesson from the cattle and trustingly drop to your knees knowing that the storm is in the hands of God Almighty?

Solomon, who understood God's intent for people, wrote in Ecclesiastes, "When times are good, be happy; but when times are bad, consider: God has made the one as well as the other. Therefore, a man cannot discover anything about his future" (7:14). What's he saying? Life is unpredictable. God won't tell us what's going to happen after the storm. He lets us wait and see. What can we do? Surrender to the storm! We can lie down in the security that the Lord allows storms at times. He also quiets them to bring peace again.

Are you facing spring storms right now? Do you feel cold and numb from the deluge? Can you "be still, and know that I am God" (Ps. 46:10)? Drop to your knees and huddle under God's protection. It's safe there.

MORE SCRIPTURE FOR STUDY:
Psalm 107:29-30; Luke 8:22-25;
Romans 5:1-5; 8:35

Wholehearted

Teach me your way, O LORD, and I will walk in your truth;
give me an undivided heart, that I may fear your name.

PSALM 86:11

THE STORY IS TOLD of a pair of swans who had been seen together in a New England town for a period of time. Perhaps they had been mates for years or only one season. Whatever the case, they exemplified a swan's behavior of mating for life. They were inseparable.

Sadly, one day the female swan died. Her mate cooed, called, and paced around her body, refusing to look for food or water. For three days he stayed with his dead mate until a townsperson caged him and brought him home. Although he continued to grieve and call, he at least began to eat again. If he had been left alone with his mate, he would have died.

That swan had an undivided heart—a heart so true to its beloved that nothing could tear it away. That is the meaning behind David's "give me an undivided heart." He wanted to have a pure heart for the Lord. Having experienced his own heart's wanderings, he knew the remorse of a heart split between God and the world. He had been torn in two by his own sin.

Like David do you also crave an intense relationship with the Lord? I do. So often my heart feels divided by fear concerning my children, anger at my spouse, discontent with my work, or frustration with my home. Will you pray with me?

Lord, give me a heart that is focused squarely on You.
Help me to love and seek You wholeheartedly.

MORE SCRIPTURE FOR STUDY:
Deuteronomy 30:6-10; Psalm 119:2-11;
Ezekiel 11:19; 1 Corinthians 13

Fishing for Faith

"Put out into deep water, and let down the nets for a catch."

LUKE 5:4

DEEP-SEA FISHING BOATS BOB ALONG the coast of New England. These "for hire" boats lure fervent fishermen out into the rough Atlantic in the hopes of catching some fish—really big fish. The claim of "deep-sea fishing" is not a misnomer either. The boats motor at least thirty miles offshore before casting a line into the depths. They go far and they go deep.

Although their passengers' enthusiasm for fishing escapes me (despite loving the ocean), I do understand the allure of the unknown depths underwater. What's down there? How silent is the silence underwater? Are there unknown leviathans—monsters of the sea (Isa. 27:1)?

Perhaps the disciples had the same questions as they fished each day for a living. I suspect theirs was a love/hate relationship with the waters in which they fished. Maybe they loved it when they caught enough to turn a profit and hated it when they spent a night of fishing with no catch to show for their efforts.

Such was the morning when Jesus used Peter's boats as a floating pulpit. (See Luke 5:1-11.) After He preached to the people on shore, He told the fishermen to go deeper and cast out the nets. They grumbled a little because they felt tired from a fruitless night. But they complied. What did they pull up besides enough fish to fill two boats? Faith with a capital *F*.

What can we learn? Sometimes we need to go a little farther and drop our nets a little deeper. In what ways? Perhaps Jesus is calling you offshore to move you away from complacency in an area of your life. Maybe He's asking you to move into a deeper relationship with someone. Will you trust Him and obey His challenge? Your reward will be a renewed and overflowing Faith.

MORE SCRIPTURE FOR STUDY:
Luke 17:5-6; 2 Corinthians 5:7;
Hebrews 11:1-2; James 2:17-18

Start Stomping

I have given you authority to trample on snakes and scorpions
and to overcome all the power of the enemy;
nothing will harm you.

LUKE 10:19

AS I LIFTED A LAUNDRY BASKET of dirty clothes to the edge of the washer, something on the floor to my right caught my eye. For a fraction of a second I thought I had seen an electrical cord. Just as quickly I realized there wasn't anything around to which a cord could be attached. Even as this thought jelled in my mind, I knew what it was: a snake. As I turned my full attention on the critter, a shiver went down my spine. Although it was just a *baby* snake, the next thought felt worse. *It must have a mother and siblings somewhere close by!* Granted, I was standing in the basement of my house, but basement or not, it was my home. I didn't like the thought of a snake family joining us. I did the only logical thing I could think of: I grabbed one of Peter's heavy loafers and cracked it on the baby snake's head.

A portion of the above verse flitted through my mind: "authority to trample on snakes." As I disposed of the little limp body outside, I checked the back-door of the house leading to the basement. Sure enough, I found a crack between the bottom edge of the door and the frame. It was just big enough for a little snake to fit through. *Whew!* I thought. *Maybe a whole family isn't inhabiting my basement.*

The same portion of Luke 10:19 came to me a second time. I had simply reacted with my instinct to kill the snake. I didn't waste time thinking about *how* to kill it, nor had I trembled with indecision about whether or not I *should* kill it. I simply took the authority to do it. No one else was going to.

If only we could act with such streamlined, decisive conviction in our faith walks. When temptation—a needling edge from the devil—slithers into our lives, how often do we survey it without taking action? Maybe we even let it build a nest right under our noses while we ponder "what to do."

What will you do in the coming days when temptation slithers your way? Take action quickly. You have the authority in God's holy name to trample right on it. Start stomping!

MORE SCRIPTURE FOR STUDY:
Psalm 60:11-12; Matthew 4:1-11;
1 Corinthians 10:13; James 1:13-15

Beauty and Thorns

See, I am setting before you today a blessing and a curse.

DEUTERONOMY 11:26

I GENTLY TWIRLED A LONG-STEMMED ROSE between my fingers, being careful not to let the thorns slice my hand. Like me, have you felt drawn by a rose's fragrance and beauty, while simultaneously feeling keenly aware of the thorns? Which do you pay more attention to: the blessing of the rose's beauty or the curse of a possible painful prick?

In the above Scripture the Lord gave the Israelites a choice. If they obeyed His commands, they would reap blessings. However, if they disobeyed His commands and worshiped other gods, they would find curses obstructing their path.

The rose I twirled reminded me of God's straightforward request. Like you, I am daily faced with the choices of exclusively following the Lord's commands or veering off track to follow "other gods." Following other gods is also known as idolatry—worshiping or giving first place to anything or anyone other than God. "Other gods" could be our homes, our jobs, our children, or our appearance. One choice leads to blessing, while the other could lead to a curse.

This week buy or pick a long-stemmed rose. Think about the Lord's promise of blessing and warning of curses. He has set them before you. Which will you choose?

MORE SCRIPTURE FOR STUDY:
Deuteronomy 11:22-32; Joshua 24:14-18;
Proverbs 10:22; Luke 10:38-42

Our God of Details

"Look at the birds of the air; they do not sow or reap or store away
in barns, and yet your heavenly Father feeds them.
Are you not much more valuable than they?"

MATTHEW 6:26

I WAS RUNNING LATE AGAIN. My "normal" time is about ten minutes late. But I feel terrible that my vice brings consequences on my children. This was my thought as I rummaged through the clean socks laundry basket (pairing them up and putting them away is another story entirely) looking for a matching set for Jordan so that I could take him to a birthday party. I quickly prayed, *Lord, help me find two socks—quick!* A second later a matching set came into view. I grabbed them, Jordan, and his shoes, and then hurried to the car. We were on our way—late.

So many times I've shot one of those heartfelt but small-detail prayers to the Lord. Simultaneously, I'll nearly apologize for being so disorganized that I even need to pray for such a detail as matching socks. Doesn't God have more important prayers to consider (i.e., a prayer for world peace)? What I've come to learn is that God listens to *all* of the prayers of His people. He doesn't prioritize them as if they flash on a giant neon sign in heaven. The Bible tells us, "by prayer and petition, with thanksgiving, present your requests to God" (Phil. 4:6). There's no addendum to this verse that says, "But only if it's a big deal."

The Lord is interested in the details of our lives. He's interested in the lives of all of His creation, judging from the above verse about the birds. He knows how many hairs are on your head, even right after you've lost a few strands in the hairbrush (Matt. 10:30)! That's our God of details. Will you trust Him to care about even the smallest details of your life?

MORE SCRIPTURE FOR STUDY:
2 Chronicles 30:23-27; Psalm 139:1-16;
Ephesians 6:18; 1 Peter 3:12

Be Sensible

Taste and see that the LORD is good; blessed is the man
who takes refuge in him.

PSALM 34:8

IMAGINE THE FRUIT THAT TEMPTED Eve. Some say an apple made her mouth water. Others aren't so certain of the actual fruit. What matters is that she saw with her eyes, heard a deceitful whisper in her ear, reached with her hand, brought the fruit to her nose to smell its sweetness, then crunched into it. Each of her senses was employed in that first sin; yet it seems she momentarily lost all of her *common sense* when she reached for the fruit!

So often we fall into the same trap Eve found herself in. Our senses trick us. Images assault our eyes and our brain decides, *I want it.* Sounds or smells trigger memories or thoughts that divert our focus.

The Lord gave us our senses as a way to understand Him better. Through our eyes we see His creation. Through our ears we hear the sounds of nature. Through our noses we smell His gardens. Through our hands we touch what He has created. Through our mouths we taste His provision. But the very tools He gave us to absorb His world are the same tools that sometimes lead us into sin.

Like Eve, do you sometimes find your senses causing you to lose your common sense? How can we influence our senses to only absorb the things of the Lord? This week pick one of your senses and concentrate on seeing, hearing, smelling, feeling, or tasting the Lord and His creation. If you pick hearing, listen for raindrops, birds, or the wind. If you pick smelling, buy a few roses or make a fruit salad and drink in the aromas. Thank God for the senses He created in you. Echo David's words: "Taste and see that the LORD is good."

MORE SCRIPTURE FOR STUDY:
Psalm 19:1-6; 119:18; Proverbs 2:1-5;
Matthew 5:6

Weeding Seedlings

First collect the weeds and tie them in bundles to be burned;
then gather the wheat and bring it into my barn.

MATTHEW 13:30

I DON'T MIND PULLING UP WEEDS in my late spring garden, but I mind very much pulling up seedlings. It seems as if the little pea plants cling to their tender roots as I rip them out. As much as I imagine a feeble cry from these plants, I know the thinning process is necessary to give the rest of the plants room enough to spread their roots.

My grandfather used to say this about pulling up healthy seedlings: "It only hurts for a moment." He philosophically advised thinning as the only way to give the other plants a good chance. This is especially true later in the growing season when carrots need thinning. If allowed to grow too close to one another, they occasionally commingle or split into forks. They're not useless this way. The deformities also won't alter the taste. A carrot, however, was created to grow straight and whole with room around it to fill out.

This is also true for our spirits. The Lord wants us to grow straight and whole. Why does the Lord pare down our seedling growth? He has the same reason as a gardener does: to allow plenty of room for good growth for an optimal chance of survival.

I may not yet have even noticed the little seedlings He is readying to pluck out of my soul. Maybe I had a flash of envy about someone's life. Maybe pride has started to mingle with my good growth. How about you? Do you notice the little seedlings that need thinning?

The Bible freely uses agricultural analogies to represent our relationship to the Lord. In the next few days, look up the verses listed below. See if you can identify yourself in one of the analogies. How are you growing in the Lord's garden?

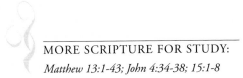

MORE SCRIPTURE FOR STUDY:
Matthew 13:1-43; John 4:34-38; 15:1-8

Changing Expectations

Accept one another, then, just as Christ accepted you,
in order to bring praise to God.

ROMANS 15:7

IN AN ONGOING EFFORT to grow strong and abundant perennial beds, one fall I planted various allegedly hardy plants that I ordered from a catalog. (Okay. That should have clued me in right there that this type of gardening might not work.) I anticipated thriving perennials in the spring despite the fact that the plants looked weak the previous winter. My expectations were not realized as spring edged into summer with still no green plants pushing through the soil.

First, I felt angry at the mail-order company. Then I felt mad at our climate and gravel-filled soil. After that I took responsibility. Maybe my expectations were at fault. Maybe where I live and the fence where I wanted a full perennial garden weren't conducive to growing a garden. Maybe *my expectations* needed to change.

Once I could apply this to my garden, I began to expand my newfound expectation philosophy. It crept into my feelings concerning relationships about which I felt discontent. It occurred to me that maybe I needed my expectations to change.

I'll bet you have those kinds of relationships too—ones that leave you feeling disappointed or short on fulfilled expectations. Maybe your spouse or children seem to "forget" your birthday or anniversary each year. Maybe a friend seems clueless about his or her role in keeping in contact with you.

If unmet expectations are an issue, there are two questions you need to ask yourself. First: "Have I communicated my expectations to the people in my life?" Second: "Are my expectations even realistic?" The second one is the clincher, isn't it? My prideful expectations fade when I ask myself that. When my expectations are unmet, it's usually because of my own unreasonably high standards.

I've decided to give up on having a lush perennial garden along one of our fences. And I'm working on releasing any unrealistic expectations I have of the people in my life. Will you join me?

MORE SCRIPTURE FOR STUDY:
Psalm 86:11; Jeremiah 7:3-8;
1 Corinthians 13:4-7;
1 Thessalonians 5:14-15

A Promise Fulfilled

I will surely bless you and make your descendants as numerous
as the stars in the sky and as the sand on the seashore.

GENESIS 22:17a

PETER, THE CHILDREN, AND I CANOED away from the shore of a fresh-water island after spending the afternoon lying on the beach and swimming. I watched the rippled sand slide by under the canoe a few feet below the water's surface. As the small bits of granite and mica caught the sun's reflected rays, the God-breathed words spoken to Abraham in Genesis rose in my mind: *I will surely bless you and make your descendants … as the sand on the seashore.*

Who among us has not walked on a beach and marveled at the immense quantity of sand all around us? The Lord didn't just mention in passing to Abraham that his descendants would be as many as the uncountable grains—He *promised* it! What's even more marvelous is that our families are a return on God's promise to Abraham. We are spiritual descendants of Abraham. What a powerful thought!

That means our lives are proof of the Lord's faithfulness. God always keeps

His word. That means we can take part in Abraham's inheritance (Gen. 22:18). That means we can count on all of God's promises. There is always an abundant return on what the Lord says. "So is my word that goes out from my mouth: it will not return empty" (Isa. 55:11). You are proof of that as a "grain" of the promised multiple descendants.

As you walk on a beach this spring or coming summer, think about your place in God's family. Will you express your thankfulness to the Lord for fulfilling His promise through you?

MORE SCRIPTURE FOR STUDY:
Deuteronomy 7:6-9; Psalm 33:9-12;
Ephesians 1:4-6; 1 Peter 2:9

The Lord Is Gracious

The LORD, the LORD, the compassionate and gracious God.

EXODUS 34:6a

Living Water

With joy you will draw water from the wells of salvation.

ISAIAH 12:3

MY MAIDEN NAME IS MARRINER. I come from sailing stock, stretching back to my Scottish great-grandfather. He was a ship's captain and a naval boat-yard builder. During my childhood and adolescence I spent summers sailing with my parents and sisters off the coast of New England and in the large inland lakes. The slap of water against a hull is in my blood. I understand the lure of the mesmerizing waves and that of distant shores.

Water is the very backbone of everyone's physical existence. It comprises about 66 percent of our bodies and is essential for our survival. No wonder Christ compared Himself to living water.

Have you ever thought about how integral water was to Christ's ministry? He was baptized in it. He changed it to wine. He healed and changed lives next to it. He walked on it. His disciples earned their living on it. He spoke and it was still. He washed His disciples' feet with it. It poured from His side when He was crucified.

Why was water so important to His ministry? It was a foretaste of the eternal living water. Jesus spoke of this water as He talked with the Samaritan woman at Jacob's well. "Indeed, the water I give him will become in him a spring of water welling up to eternal life" (John 4:14b). What did He mean by "living"? This water would never stagnate or run dry, nor would it ever cease flowing. Instead it would always be refreshing, always available, always cleansing.

Our spiritual lives can feel either dry and dusty or like a refreshing dip in cool water. How will you face this coming summer? Will you draw from the well of Christ's living water in God's holy Word to keep your soul hydrated and refreshed?

MORE SCRIPTURE FOR STUDY:
Isaiah 58:11; John 4:1-42;
Hebrews 10:19, 22; 1 John 5:6-12

Willing to Be Led

*Do not be stiff-necked any longer. For the LORD your God is
God of gods and Lord of lords, the great God,
mighty and awesome, who shows no impartiality.*

DEUTERONOMY 10:16-17

RIDING AND HANDLING ONE OF MY HORSES, Foxfyre, has shown me
what being stiff-necked is like. Iron-necked is more like it. She must have
stubborn mule in her lineage. When she decides she's not going to do something, her neck stiffens.

One summer, after two previous years of work to clear, seed, and fertilize a
new grazing field for the horses, I set about moving the horses to their new
pasture. But Foxfyre planted her feet and stiffened her neck. She would not
be coerced or tricked into moving from the spot to which she'd rooted herself.
I pointed out to her that the rock-growing, no-grass-in-sight, broken-down
paddock could be her home no longer. Lush grass awaited her in the new pasture. It would satisfy her hunger. No longer would she have to eat hay. She
remained unconvinced, however.

I saw myself mirrored in Foxfyre's stubbornness. How about you? Ever feel stiff-necked when the Lord points you in a new direction? Ever feel stuck in a routine simply because it is familiar?

We often feel safe in our broken-down spirits because they require little effort to remain that way. But the Lord promises us the desires of our hearts (Ps. 37:4), complete contentment (Prov. 19:23), and hungers satisfied (Ps. 107:9). How can He fulfill His promise if we stubbornly refuse to move to the places He has prepared for us?

We need to learn to relax our necks a bit. We need to stretch out those stiffened muscles and allow ourselves to be led to a better, more fulfilling place. Did you catch that? *Led.* The Lord will not point a finger and send us ahead alone. He will always remain by our sides with a gentle hand on our stiff muscles, leading us step by step closer to the land He has ready for us— "a land flowing with milk and honey" (Exod. 3:8).

MORE SCRIPTURE FOR STUDY:
Exodus 34:8-10; Isaiah 40:11;
Acts 7:44-51; 2 Corinthians 2:14

Group Effect

Let us not give up meeting together ... but
let us encourage one another.

HEBREWS 10:25

LILACS ARE ONE OF MY FAVORITE early summer flowers. The sweet aroma takes me back to my childhood home where a gigantic hedge of lilac served as a hiding place for my sisters and me.

We spent hours together among the delicate purple flowers, braiding them into each other's hair, setting up dollhouses among the gnarled trunks, and even sucking a tiny drop of liquid from the stem of each tender flower.

A couple of years ago I uprooted two healthy lilac bushes from my grandmother's house and transplanted them along our backyard fence. I hoped to rekindle my childhood memories through the aroma of lilacs. But the following spring only one lilac branch held a lone bunch of the flowers. How disappointed I felt! I wanted a full hedge now! A single sprig looked lonely, desolate, and ineffective compared with the full hedge I had hoped for.

I could feel a lesson brewing. We're also less effective when we try to accomplish the Lord's work independently of other people. Although we can have an impact as individuals, we often have a greater impact as a group.

Paul's words, "Let us not give up meeting together," remind us that we work better as a group. Like a bouquet of flowers that brightens an entire room and fills it with sweet fragrance (as opposed to a single bloom that struggles to be seen), we leave a greater impression when we work in groups. We aren't meant to be Lone Rangers in our faith. The Lord designed us to complement one another in our giftedness and skills.

Are there areas in your life where you're trying to have an impact as a single bloom? Have you prayed for or sought out like-minded people with whom you can work? The Lord tells us that He is present with groups working together in His name. "I tell you that if two of you on earth agree about anything you ask for, it will be done for you by my Father in heaven. For where two or three come together in my name, there am I with them" (Matt. 18:19-20). Pray for opportunities to use your gifts to minister in a group. You may be surprised by what can be achieved through united effort.

MORE SCRIPTURE FOR STUDY:
Ecclesiastes 4:9-12; Joel 2:15-16;
Matthew 12:30; 1 Corinthians 12:12-31

Whose Plans?

God had planned something better for us so that only together with us would they be made perfect.

HEBREWS 11:40

OUR HOUSE WAS BUILT as a summer cottage for an elderly couple from Florida. We bought it knowing how much work winterizing it and making it a year-round home would take. We had a vision for the remodeling. The interior was stripped, a kitchen built, walls put up, the roof torn off to add another floor, woods cleared, and a barn built. The problem, however, is that we're still remodeling twelve years later. Over the years we have considered or sketched out various plans for our house and property. With each successive idea, we trashed the previous one.

I've come to realize how good it was that we didn't follow through on those plans. Each succeeding idea has certainly been better than the last and seemed to contain a broader vision of the future. Yet finances have usually thwarted our ideas before they even get past the drawing table. Our plans are big, but our wallet is thin.

It's easy to feel frustrated when plans are overturned. So we prayerfully ask the Lord why each plan gets trashed before it comes into being. His answer is always simple: "I have a better plan." He's really protecting us from ourselves when the door closes on our plans. He knows that when left to our own dreams and devices, we completely mess up. But His stop sign is more than a protective measure. He stops us to allow His *perfect* plan to come to pass at the right time.

I'm so grateful to know that God has the best plan waiting for us. We haven't even thought of it yet! How about you? Do you have plans that seem to fizzle or result in a slammed door? Jeremiah 29:11 says, "'For I know the plans I have for you,' declares the LORD, 'plans to prosper you and not harm you, plans to give you hope and a future.'" His promised plan is always better than ours because it guarantees us hope in His timely future. I can wait for that. Can you?

MORE SCRIPTURE FOR STUDY:
Job 42:1-6; Psalm 40:4-8; Proverbs 19:21; Isaiah 46:9-11

Storytelling

"He who has ears, let him hear."

MATTHEW 11:15

NATIVE AMERICANS IN THE NORTHEAST (as well as other parts of the country) had stories and explanations for everything. They "read" nature around them and created stories for explanations. Mount Monadnock in New Hampshire represented strength and dignity. Lake Winnipesaukee, the largest lake in New Hampshire, gave them food and water. Rock outcroppings in lakes each held a story about a family or, as in Squam Lake, of lost love. Giant oaks and elms marked the passage of time.

Humans have a basic need for explanations. The Lord created us with a curious nature and a desire to understand. Why else have we had the advancement of technology, medicine, and science? We weren't content with the status quo. We wanted an improved understanding of our world around us and, more importantly, ourselves.

Jesus understood our basic need for understanding. That's why He used parables to teach the disciples and us through the Word. Parables tell a story that parallels our lives like two tracks running side by side with the same destination.

The Bible takes on a very personal tone when we read stories about the universal human condition, doesn't it? Jesus didn't always instruct by preaching. He often taught through storytelling. He used word pictures so that we could indeed *see* what He was talking about. Page through a red-letter edition of the Bible. How about reading a few of those stories in the coming days and taking note of how they parallel your life?

MORE SCRIPTURE FOR STUDY:
Nehemiah 8:8; Matthew 13:1-52;
Colossians 2:2-3

Tenacity

Never be lacking in zeal, but keep your spiritual fervor,
serving the Lord.

ROMANS 12:11

DANDELIONS ARE THE BANE of every lawn. These cheery, yellow-headed flowers crouch close to the ground and multiply without abandon. Their determination finds them rooted in city sidewalks, on airport runways, and in the poorest sections of our country. Drought, traffic, or even the human desire to be rid of them does not affect them. Their nature is resilient. They have a zeal to grow and multiply.

Now consider the rose. Fragrant blossoms are the hope of every gardener. The tender petals, translucent alone but forming a thick foliage together, are cultivated to grow in a rainbow of colors. But these finicky bushes require gentle, knowledgeable hands. Roses need to be carefully nurtured and pruned.

If people were flowers, which type would be more useful to the Lord: the dandelion or the rose? I would venture to say the dandelion. Not that the Lord can't use the persnickety nature of a rose—their beauty certainly draws admirers. But a dandelion perseveres in hardship and stubbornly digs its roots deeper when threatened.

Consider Paul's words in 2 Timothy: "But you, keep your head in all situations, endure hardship, do the work of an evangelist, discharge all the duties of your ministry" (4:5). Let's take a lesson from the dandelion. Let's form a deep and abiding root system in Christ. Let's store up living water in our souls for times of drought. Let's multiply, filling our neighborhoods with the joy of growing in Christ.

This week, watch for dandelions along your routes to and from work, home, church, and appointments. Ask the Lord to plant in you a desire to be like the dandelions.

MORE SCRIPTURE FOR STUDY:

Romans 5:1-5;

1 Corinthians 9:16-19; 13:4-7;

2 Timothy 2:1-7

Contentment

"Consider how the lilies grow. They do not labor or spin.
Yet I tell you, not even Solomon in all his splendor
was dressed like one of these."

LUKE 12:27

HAVE YOU EVER SEEN a flower fret? Are they discontented with what they were created to be? Have you ever heard a tulip say to a rose, "Hey, Rosie, I wish I looked like you. I'd love to have people admire my buds and indulge their noses with a refreshing whiff"? Ever hear the rose say to the tulip, "Boy, Neighbor, I would love to be a tulip—tall and straight with no thorns but with perfectly cupped petals to catch the rain. Man, I wish I were you"?

How ridiculous! (Think about the nature of both. Who really wants to be either? The rose has piercing thorns and a tulip's life is short.) Yet isn't that exactly what we do? We look at our neighbors or friends and whisper behind a cupped hand, "Wouldn't I just love to have a house like that!" or "I wish I had Tom's enthusiastic personality."

What's behind this? Discontentment. I see it so blatantly in my life. When

I look at a friend's prolific garden or a neighbor's sprawling house, I feel a discontented crankiness settle over me. Frequently it seems to me that the grass really is greener on the Joneses' side of the fence.

Yet Jesus tells us to take a lesson from the lilies. They don't fret or toss and turn about what they are or aren't. They just grow and fulfill their time in season as the Lord created them to do.

Paul says in Philippians, "I have learned to be content whatever the circumstances" (4:11). As he suggests, contentment is a learning process. Learning starts with a desire to be taught. If you're stuck in discontentment, do you want to continue to fret and feed on its bitter root? Or will you choose to look at your neighbor's yard, car, children, job, etc. and say aloud, "I am learning to be content. Thank You, Lord, that I do not have to compare myself to anyone. I know Your purpose for *me* will be fulfilled" (see Romans 8:28)?

MORE SCRIPTURE FOR STUDY:
Psalm 90:14; Ecclesiastes 5:10-20;
1 Timothy 6:6-8

False Eyes

"There is no truth in [the devil]. When he lies, he speaks his native language, for he is a liar and the father of lies."

JOHN 8:44b

THE LORD PLACED the protection of camouflage in His creation, from the tawny grass color of lions to dappled newborn fawns. Have you noticed that not only are some of His tiniest creations camouflaged, but they are masters at deception too? For example, take a look at the Emperor moth. When its frail but giant wings are folded together, its segmented body is exposed—just a quick crunch for a passing bird. But when he opens his wings, four black bull's-eye centers rimmed in white unfold. The daunting look of these four "giant eyes" deceives his predator. The pretend eyes look as if they belong to a larger creature that could easily eat the bird itself. The bird wings on, looking for smaller prey. The moth continues his deception and lives for another day.

A beautiful, harmless moth can't be compared to the sneaky devil, but its self-preservation tactics can. The devil also presents himself in a form other than his true identity. He tries to trick us into thinking he's bigger and more powerful than our Lord is. He tries to look other than what he is—a cheater and a liar.

In the Gospel of John, Jesus compared the Pharisees' dishonest tactics with those of the devil. The devil tries to deceive by masking the truth. But we can learn to recognize him in different forms. Maybe he's whispering in your ear every time you pass your attractive coworker's desk. Or maybe he's in disguise in the plate of cookies that you can't stop eating and eating and eating.

You have the ability see him for what he is. Take a closer look at his deceptions. Notice how his disguises just cover up his weakness in comparison to Christ. He can be tricky, but he doesn't have to trick you.

MORE SCRIPTURE FOR STUDY:
Proverbs 14:5-8; Romans 16:17-20;
Galatians 2:4-6; Ephesians 5:6-17

Renovations

The builder of a house has greater honor than the house itself.
For every house is built by someone, but God is
the builder of everything.

HEBREWS 3:3b-4

ONE OF THE FAVORITE ADAGES of our state reads: "Welcome to New Hampshire. If you don't like the weather, wait five minutes." The weather is as subject to change as a two-year-old's moods. That's why historic New England homes were built with three- to four-foot thick granite foundations, walls a foot thick, and inch-thick glass panes. These precautions were for longevity and to keep the weather out.

For two centuries many of these houses have been subject to repeated frosts and thaws, hurricanes, droughts, heat waves, and the occasional minor earthquake. The impact of the weather shows in the houses' warped siding, skewed foundations, and unyielding windows.

Yet historic old homes are among the most popular types of houses to buy in New England. From the quaint Cape Cod, to the traditional Colonial, to the sprawling Federal style—people want a taste of the past now. Buyers beware, however; old New England houses have the highest upkeep in maintenance. It's guaranteed that *something* will always need fixing.

Sounds like our faith, doesn't it? Something always needs fixing. Maybe we need to patch up a broken friendship. Or perhaps we need to strip a decaying area for new material to be added later. Maybe we need to shore up our sinking foundation and develop a stronger one in the Lord.

Just as there is no such thing as status quo with an old house, there can be no status quo in our relationship with the Lord. He always wants to fix us up, with the goal of making us spiritually sound.

Do you have high maintenance areas in your life? Confess them to the Lord. Ask Him to begin a new work in you—to restore you to what He wants you to be.

MORE SCRIPTURE FOR STUDY:
Matthew 7:24-27; Philippians 1:5-6;
Hebrews 12:1-2; 1 Peter 2:5

Nurturing the Lost

"If a man owns a hundred sheep, and one of them wanders away,
will he not leave the ninety-nine on the hills and go
to look for the one that wandered off?"

MATTHEW 18:12

DURING THE FIRST YEAR that we raised chickens for meat, one of the birds obviously was not well. It couldn't stand or walk. It flapped its wings helplessly, sometimes with enough force to turn itself in a circle.

A true farmer would put the bird out of its misery with a sharp ax on a chopping block. After all, the chickens are destined for the freezer. But I'm an animal lover. I felt I had to try to do something to help it. My motivation didn't spring from saving the bird because I wanted the meat. I was motivated simply to help a suffering animal. Besides, its eyes looked bright as it pecked eagerly at the grain in my hand.

I checked with a poultry lab about why the chicken couldn't walk. It seemed likely that he had been malnourished at a critical growing phase. His leg tendons just couldn't support his fast-growing body weight.

So I nurtured the bird. I hand-fed him four times a day and made sure that he could reach fresh water. I chased the other chickens away from him and placed him in the sun each day for fresh air. My maternal instincts had been stirred. By the end of the growing time, my pet chicken could stand for short periods of time and totter to the feeder on his own. I couldn't have felt happier.

It sounds a bit like the parable of the lost sheep, doesn't it? Jesus said the shepherd is happier about finding the lost sheep than about the ninety-nine waiting on the hill. My ailing chicken helped me to understand what Jesus meant when He said, "In the same way your Father in heaven is not willing that any of these little ones should be lost" (Matt. 18:14).

The Lord is not willing for any of us to be spiritually ill or lost. To Him we are never in a hopeless situation. He stubbornly refuses to let us stay lost or weak. He will nurture us individually, hand-feed us spiritual food when we're sick, and stand guard over us. He is not satisfied until we are healthy and back in the safety of His sheepfold.

MORE SCRIPTURE FOR STUDY:
Psalms 5:11-12; 91:14-16; Isaiah 53:6;
Ezekiel 34:11-16

Faith in Flesh

Since ancient times no one has heard, no ear has perceived,
no eye has seen any God besides you,
who acts on behalf of those who wait for him.

ISAIAH 64:4

MY SON JORDAN wanted a puppy. When he was only four, he picked out the name. When he was five, he decided he wanted a golden retriever. When he was six, he started crying himself to sleep, so desperate for a certain soul mate.

At one point in Jordan's young life, we had three dogs. But once the two older dogs died, I really liked having just one. Yet Jordan wore me down. So, when he was eight, we bought Tupper Lake, a golden retriever.

He turned out to be a great puppy. He trained easily and seemed pleased with himself when he did something right. But puppies are known to do two things unerringly: urinate indiscriminately and chew. We got the first one under control pretty quickly. The chewing was a different story.

No matter how many squeaky, chewy, soft, hard, big, or small chew toys I bought him, he stuck with one preference: our feet or hands. He stayed unimpressed with my increasingly expensive diversions for him. The truth was that he needed flesh.

He really just expressed his wild instincts. Flesh can feed; rubber can't. Flesh will nourish; a tennis ball won't. This instinct in dogs is really no different than the one for us humans. We're born needing a mother's milk delivered through her flesh. As we grow, the protein from the meat of animals nourishes us.

But we have an even deeper hunger. Our greatest need is for God in the flesh—Jesus Christ. "The Word became flesh and made his dwelling among us" (John 1:14a). The Word is God Himself. Why did Jesus have to take on flesh? Nothing else would do. Nothing but the death of Christ's physical body could purge us of sin. The knowledge that He lived in a body like ours and can identify with us in every way sustains us.

In the coming days, dwell on what Christ's coming in the flesh has meant for you spiritually. Could anything less than the death of a sinless man accomplish God's purpose to forgive sins?

MORE SCRIPTURE FOR STUDY:
John 3:16; Romans 5:6-11;
1 Corinthians 15:20-22; 1 Peter 2:1-3

Alike in Differences

As for those who seemed to be important—whatever they were makes no difference to me; God does not judge by external appearance.

GALATIANS 2:6a

A ROSE IS A ROSE is a rose. In a fundamental way, they are all the same. But some are climbers, while others are low to the ground. Some have thick, cutting thorns; others have little pricks. A few thrive in the North; others prefer the South. But they're all still roses, discernible by their vivid aroma and tightly cupped petals.

Could the same be said of humans? The Lord created us with vastly different genetic makeups evidenced in our facial features, body types, hair, and—most distinguishing—our fingerprints.

But like the roses, we are alike in a fundamental way. This is described in Romans 3:23: "For all have sinned and fall short of the glory of God." Although we differ in physical appearance, we all are the same in the appearance of our souls. We are tainted with sin. Sin is sin is sin. Although sin displays itself in varying forms—from untruths to murder—it's still sin. It's still the antithesis of the purity of God.

We are alike in another way. When we believe that Jesus died to pay the price for our sins, we're given the gift of eternal life (John 3:16). As David wrote, "He does not treat us as our sins deserve or repay us according to our iniquities" (Ps. 103:10). Why? In God's eyes, we're worth saving. He created us. Seeing the destruction of His creation hurts Him.

In the coming days and weeks, really *look* at the people around you. It's so easy to focus on how people are different from us and feel intolerant of what we see. Instead, try to remember how everyone is the same in God's eyes: worth dying for.

MORE SCRIPTURE FOR STUDY:
Isaiah 1:18; Romans 2:1; Ephesians 4:1-6;
1 John 1:5-10

All Things Bright and Beautiful

All things bright and beautiful,
All creatures great and small,
All things wise and wonderful,
The Lord God made them all.

Each little flower that opens,
Each little bird that sings,
He made their glowing colors;
He made their tiny wings.

The purple-headed mountains,
The river running by,
The sunset and the morning
That brightens up the sky.

The cold wind in the winter,
The pleasant summer sun,
The ripe fruits in the garden:
God made them every one.

He gave us eyes to see them,
And lips that we might tell
How great is God Almighty,
Who has made all things well.

CECIL FRANCES ALEXANDER

A NATIVE NEW ENGLANDER, Elizabeth Hoekstra lives on a farm in southern New Hampshire with her husband, Peter, and their two children. She holds an R.N. degree, with a concentration in psychology and maternal health, and has worked in both hospital and community health settings. Currently she manages Direct Path Ministries, which encourages women and families to form deeper interpersonal relationships under the lordship of Jesus Christ. Elizabeth also gardens, shows her horse Galilee, and enjoys skiing, boating, kayaking, biking, and hiking with her family.

Other Crossway books by Elizabeth M. Hoekstra

Keeping Your Family Close When Frequent Travel Pulls You Apart

Just for Girls

Just for Moms

A Season of Rejoicing

A Season of Grace

A Season of Stillness

With Mary Bradford
Chronic Kids, Constant Hope

MARLENE M^cLOUGHLIN WAS BORN IN BUFFALO, NEW YORK, and grew up in southern California. She received a degree in art history from Barnard College in New York City and a degree in drawing "with high distinction" from California College of Arts and Crafts.

In 1998 she went to Rome to work on her book *Road to Rome* (Chronicle Books) and decided to stay because of the beauty of the landscape and because dogs are allowed almost everywhere. She lives with Kiddo, a tortoise shell cat, and Barely, a German-Italian shepherd mix … both pets are bilingual!

Marlene works from home on projects that vary from logo design to wall paintings. Her internationally award-winning books include: *Diane Seed's Rome for All Seasons, Across the Aegean,* and *The Passionate Observer.* Her clients include Linda Ronstadt, Williams-Sonoma, Ten Speed Press, and HarperCollins.

The typeface for this book is Adobe Garamond, originally designed by Claude Garamond in 1532. His oldstyle designs, based on the Aldine model, were the typefaces of choice in the composing rooms of printers well into the 18th century. In 1989 Robert Slimbach modified the design of this typeface slightly for Adobe, and it remains a favorite for book designers today.

The script used throughout is Escrita, a three weight, hand-drawn face designed by Mário Feliciano for T-26 in 1997.

The interior for this series was set by Joe Rosewell and Rose Graham.